STEP ONE:

Play Blues Guitar

by Darryl Winston

Master basic blues guitar. Put on the CD to hear each technique and tune, then play along! Easily learn the basics of chords, strums, and fingerpicking as you step into the exciting world of blues guitar.

T0070822

Cover instrument owned by Scot Arch
Photographed by William H. Draffen

This book Copyright © 1997 by Amsco Publications,
A Division of Music Sales Corporation, New York

All rights reserved. No part of this book may be
reproduced in any form or by any electronic or mechanical means,
including information storage and retrieval systems,
without permission in writing from the publisher.

Order No. AM 942040
US International Standard Book Number: 0.8256.1591.7
UK International Standard Book Number: 0.7119.6282.0

Exclusive Distributors:
Music Sales Limited
Distribution Centre, Newmarket Road, Bury St Edmunds, Suffolk IP33 3YB, UK.
Music Sales Corporation
180 Madison Avenue, 24th Floor, New York NY 10016, USA.
Music Sales Pty Limited
Units 3-4, 17 Willfox St, Condell Park, NSW, 2200 Australia

Printed in Great Britain

Amsco Publications
New York/London/Sydney

CD Track List

1	Introduction
2	Blues Chords in A
3	Blues Pattern in A
4	The Twelve-Bar Blues in A
5	Blues Chords in E
6	Blues Pattern in E
7	C.C. Rider
8	Strum Patterns (The A Chord)
9	Strum Pattern Variations
10	Worried Man Blues
11	Bass-Chord Strum Patterns
12	Goin' Down That Road Feelin' Bad
13	Bass-Chord Strum Pattern Variations
14	Reading Guitar Tablature (the E Pentatonic Blues Scale)
15	Hammerons, Pulloffs, Slides, and Bends
16	Fills and Turnarounds
17	Fill Variations
18	Turnaround Chords
19	Turnaround Solo Riff
20	Corinna, Corinna
21	Intros and Endings
22	Intro Solo Riffs
23	Ending Chord Pattern
24	Ending Solo Riff
25	Chilly Wind Blues
26	Solo Technique
27	Riff Variations
28	Stagolee
29	Improvising Riffs
30	Midnight Special
31	Minor Blues
32	St. James Infirmary
33	Country Blues
34	Risin' River Blues
35	Jazz Blues
36	St. Louis Blues
37	Rock Blues
38	Crossroad Blues
39	Conclusion

Contents

Introduction 4

Blues Chords in A 5
   The Twelve-Bar Blues 5

Blues Chords in E 6
   C.C. Rider 6

Strum Patterns 7
   Worried Man Blues 7

Bass-Chord Strum Patterns 8
   Goin' Down That Road Feelin' Bad 8

Reading Guitar Tablature 9

Hammerons, Pulloffs, Slides, and Bends 9

Fills and Turnarounds 10
   Corinna, Corinna 11

Intros and Endings 13
   Chill Wind Blues 14

Solo Technique 15
   Stagolee 16

Improvising Riffs 18
   Midnight Special 19

Minor Blues 21
   St. James Infirmary 21

Country Blues 24
   Risin' River Blues 24

Jazz Blues 26
   St. Louis Blues 27

Rock Blues 29
   Crossroad Blues 30

Table of Blues Scales 32

Table of Blues Chords 34

Introduction

The guitar is the single most important instrument in the history of the blues—and it continues to define the sound of blues and rock today. The instrument's versatility and expressive power make it a natural choice for blues improvisation—and a superb complement to the human voice. In fact, the blues began as a vocal form which grew out of the work songs and spirituals written by African-American slaves. Early blues guitarists discovered how to use techniques such as slides, bends, and vibrato to imitate blues singers. With this exciting new vocabulary, together with a strong sense of personal style, they brought the instrument—and the blues itself—to new heights of expression.

Whether you are a beginning guitarist, or an experienced player, this easy instruction guide contains everything you need to know to master the basics of blues guitar. You'll learn blues chords, progressions, and scales in every key—and explore classic blues fills, turnarounds, intros, and endings. You'll also get to create your own solos and riffs using important blues techniques, such as hammerons, pulloffs, slides, and bends. Useful fingerpicking and strum patterns are also provided, along with suggestions for developing your own blues accompaniments. For easy reading, the examples and songs in this book are shown in both music notation and guitar tablature.

As you learn new blues patterns and techniques, you'll get to perform a variety of a classic blues songs in different styles. These songs are favorites of many great blues players, including Mississippi John Hurt, Blind Lemon Jefferson, Mance Lipscomb, Robert Johnson, Furry Lewis, Dave Van Ronk, Eric Clapton, Leadbelly, and Woody Guthrie. You will also find special sections on country, jazz, and rock blues—and get a chance to explore some of the techniques used by the masters of these styles.

Once you are familiar with the basics of the blues, you will be able to play hundreds of new songs on your own. In fact, exploring new songs and techniques is the best way to develop your own personal playing style. It also helps to listen to the work of the blues masters—and to create opportunities to practice and perform with other blues musicians.

Blues Chords in A

A basic blues requires only three chords—the I7, IV7, and V7 chords of a given major key. These chords are built on the first, fourth, and fifth degrees of a major scale. In the key of A, the basic blues chords are A7, D7, and E7. This is a favorite key of many blues guitarists because it is easy and natural sounding. The following *chord diagrams* show how these three chords are fingered on the guitar fretboard.

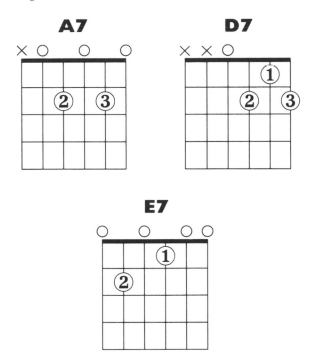

The Twelve-Bar Blues

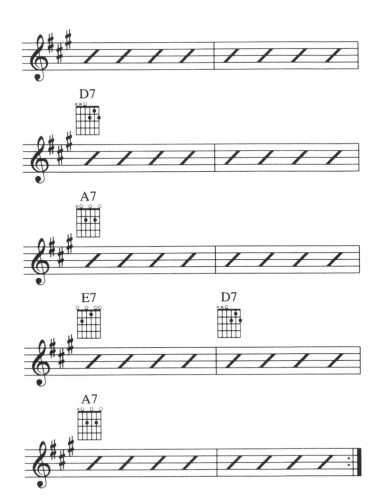

Practice playing these chords in this pattern, strumming each chord four times, as shown. Repeat this pattern several times in tempo.

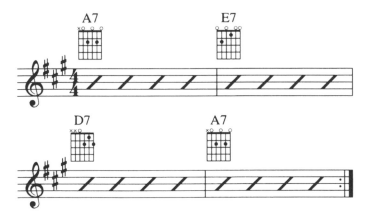

Once you can change from one chord to another smoothly and easily, try playing the *twelve-bar blues progression* that follows. This chord pattern is the basic form for thousands of standard blues songs.

Blues Chords in E

In the key of E, the three basic blues chords are E7, A7, and B7, which are built on the first, fourth, and fifth degrees of the E Major Scale. You are already familiar with the A7 and E7 chords. Play them again now along with the B7 chord.

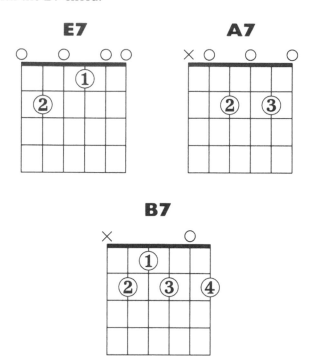

Practice playing these chords in this pattern, strumming each chord four times, as shown. Repeat this pattern several times in tempo.

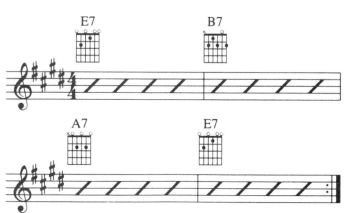

Once you can change from one chord to another smoothly and easily, try playing "C.C. Rider" in the key of E. This classic song was often performed by blues guitarists Mississippi John Hurt and Mance Lipscomb. Also known as "See See Rider," this traditional American blues became a a chart hit for a wide range of blues, R&B, and rock artists, including Ma Rainey (1925), Chuck Willis (1957), Lavern Baker (1963), and Eric Burdon & the Animals (1966).

C.C. Rider

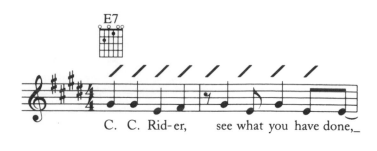

2. C.C. Rider, I need you by my side,
I said, C.C. Rider, I need you by my side.
You're the only one who keeps me satisfied.

3. Goin' away, Rider, won't be back till fall,
Yes, I'm goin' away, Rider, won't be back till fall.
If I find some good love, won't be back at all.

© 1993 Music Sales Corporation (ASCAP)
International Copyright Secured. All Rights Reserved.

Strum Patterns

Now that you've learned the blues chords in two important keys, get ready to play some different strum patterns. Traditional blues guitarists use different *fingerstyle strums* to add interest and movement to their playing. Until now, you have played four even strums per measure using downstrokes. Try this on an A chord now.

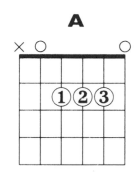

You can make your accompaniment more interesting by adding upstrokes in between the four main downstrokes in each measure. Use your right-hand fingers to brush down and up on an A chord using this strum pattern.

■ = downstroke
V = upstroke

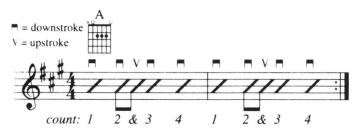

Here are three variations on this strum that you can use to add interest at different points in a blues song.

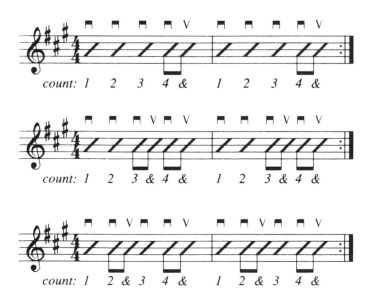

Now play "Worried Man Blues" using the indicated strum patterns. This old song is a particular favorite of bluegrass and country players—and features a sixteen-bar blues form (an extended version of the twelve-bar blues). Once you can play "Worried Man Blues" smoothly as written, play the song a few more times and explore some strum patterns of your own.

Worried Man Blues

2. I went across the river and laid me down to sleep, *(3 times)*
   When I woke up, I had shackles on my feet.

3. Twenty-nine links of chain around my leg,
   On each link, an initial of my name.

4. I asked the judge, what might be my fine,
   Twenty-one years on the Rocky Mountain line.

© 1993 Music Sales Corporation (ASCAP)
International Copyright Secured. All Rights Reserved.

Bass-Chord Strum Patterns

Many blues guitarists use *broken chords* to add a hard-driving, rhythmic quality to their playing. The simplest broken-chord pattern is called the *bass-chord strum*. For this strum, play a single bass note with the thumb on the first beat of each measure and then strum downward on all the other strings with the fingers three times in tempo. Try this pattern using the A7 and E7 chords. Use your thumb to play string ⑤ for the A7 chord bass note and string ⑥ for the E7 chord bass note, as indicated. Repeat this pattern several times in tempo.

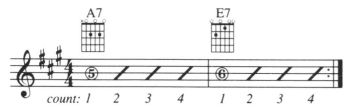

Now play "Goin' Down That Road Feelin' Bad" using this pattern. This traditional blues song was made famous by Woody Guthrie—and is featured in the repertoire of many blues and country-blues musicians. Like "Worried Man Blues," this one has a sixteen-bar blues form. Feel free to sing the melody (or have a friend sing or play it) as you practice a steady bass-chord accompaniment. Once you can play "Goin' Down That Road Feelin' Bad" smoothly as written, play the song a few more times and explore the following variations on the bass-chord strum.

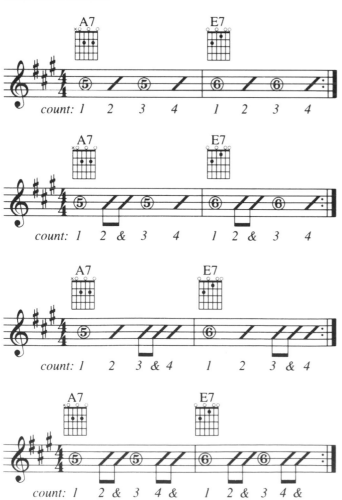

Goin' Down That Road Feelin' Bad

2. Takes a ten-dollar shoe to fit my feet, *(3 times)*
   Lord, Lord, and I ain't gonna be treated this-a-way.

3. 'Cause your two-dollar shoes hurt my feet,
   Lord, Lord, and I ain't gonna be treated this-a-way.

4. I'm goin' where the weather suits my clothes,
   Lord, Lord, no I ain't gonna be treated this-a-way.

© 1993 Music Sales Corporation (ASCAP)
International Copyright Secured. All Rights Reserved.

Reading Guitar Tablature

Tablature is a well-known system of notation designed specially for guitarists. The tablature staff is composed of six lines. Each line represents a string of the guitar, with string **1** being the highest, and string **6**, the lowest.

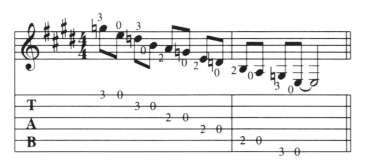

Fret numbers placed on the lines of guitar tablature tell you which fret to play on a given string. (Fret **1** is the fret nearest to the tuning pegs and **0** indicates an unfretted or *open string*.) When fingering numbers are included, they appear with the notes on the staff: 1=index finger, 2=middle finger, 3=ring finger, and 4=pinky.

The first-position *E pentatonic blues scale* is shown below in music notation and guitar tablature. Play this descending scale several times in tempo. Use your middle finger (2) for notes on the second fret and your ring finger (3) for notes on the third fret, as indicated.

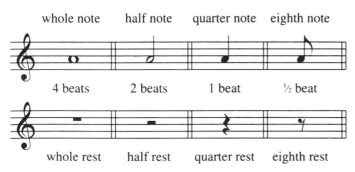

While guitar tablature shows you which frets and strings to play, you must get the rhythm from the notes on the music staff. Here are four standard note values and rests—and their relative duration in beats.

Now play the same descending E pentatonic blues scale in a new rhythmic pattern as you count aloud.

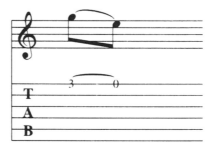

Hammerons, Pulloffs, Slides, and Bends

Hammeron. A slur connecting two ascending notes indicates a hammeron. Play the open first string. While the note is sounding, bring the ring finger (3) of your left hand down at the third fret to play the second note.

Pulloff. A slur connecting two descending notes indicates a pulloff. Fret the first string with your ring finger (3) at the third fret—then play the first note. While the note is still ringing, pluck the string with your left-hand third finger to sound the open-string note.

Slide. A slur and a diagonal line between two notes indicates a slide. Fret the third string with your middle finger (2) at the second fret. Then play the note and quickly slide this finger up the string to the fourth fret.

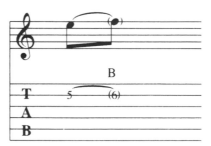

Bend. A slur (with the letter **B**) connecting two notes indicates a bend. Fret the second string with your ring finger (3) at the fifth fret—and play the first note. While the note is sounding, push the string upward to bend the pitch up to the higher note (shown in parentheses).

Fills and Turnarounds

A *fill* is a short instrumental section that occurs at the end of each line of the blues. A *turnaround* is a special type of fill used at the end of each verse, which leads naturally to the beginning of the next verse.

Corinna, Corinna, where you been so long? *(fill)*
Corinna, Corinna, where you been so long? *(fill)*
I ain't had no lovin' since you been gone.   *(turnaround)*

Here's a fill which is based on the pentatonic blues scale in the key of E. Use your middle finger (2) for notes on the second fret and your ring finger (3) for notes on the third fret.

You can create many effective fills using the notes of the pentatonic blues scale. Here are some other useful fills in the key of E to practice.

Most turnarounds use the V7 chord during the last measure of a song to "turn around" the harmony and prepare our ears for the I chord at the beginning of the next verse. Play the E, Am, and C7 chords, then strum this classic turnaround progression in the key of E.

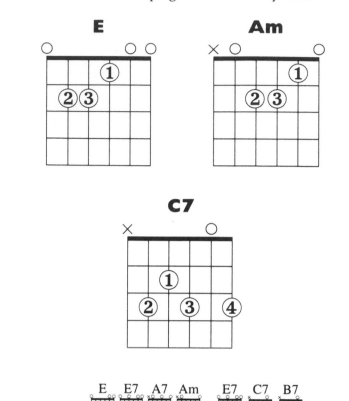

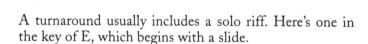

A turnaround usually includes a solo riff. Here's one in the key of E, which begins with a slide.

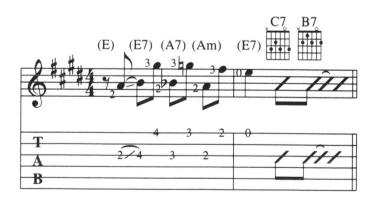

Now play "Corinna, Corinna" with the indicated strums, fills, and turnarounds. This traditional African-American blues has been recorded by many blues, country, and swing artists—and became a chart hit for Ray Peterson in 1961. Once you can play this old-time blues smoothly as written, play the song a few more times and explore alternate fills and turnarounds (or make up some of your own).

Corinna, Corinna

© 1993 Music Sales Corporation (ASCAP)
International Copyright Secured. All Rights Reserved.

Cor-in-na, Cor-in-na, where'd you stay last night?

Your shoes ain't but-toned, girl, don't fit you right.

Intros and Endings

Traditional blues guitarists often play an instrumental *introduction* before the song begins. This is a nice place to do some solo work and establish the mood. The classic blues intro echoes the harmony of the last line of the song itself. Here's an intro progression for a twelve-bar blues in the key of A. Strum this one now.

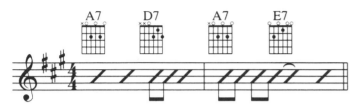

An intro usually includes a solo riff. Strum and play this intro in the key of A, which features a bluesy bend. The groups of three eighth notes are called *triplets*. Play each group in the space of one beat to lend an easygoing *shuffle* feeling to this riff.

Here's another two-bar intro with a shuffle feel. To play this one, hold over the first note of each triplet, as shown.

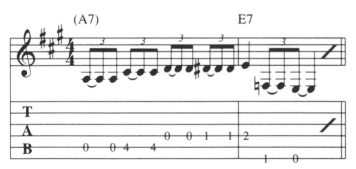

This rhythm is usually indicated as a quarter note and an eighth note grouped together with a triplet bracket.

Most blues songs end with a two-measure chord progression, finishing on the I7 chord. Certain minor chords can be very effective in the typical blues ending. Play the D minor chord, then strum this classic ending progression in the key of A.

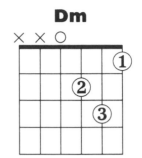

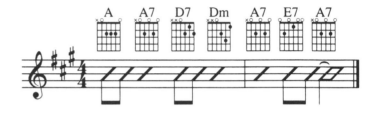

An ending can also include a solo riff. Strum and play this one in the key of A.

The shuffle rhythm can also be used when strumming chords. In fact, most blues songs are played with this easygoing feel.

Now play "Chilly Wind Blues" in a shuffle rhythm with the indicated intro and ending. The symbol at the top of the arrangement tells you to play each pair of eighth notes in the triplet pattern shown.

Once you can play "Chilly Wind Blues" smoothly as written, play the song a few more times and invent your own intros and endings.

Chilly Wind Blues

Medium shuffle (♩♩ = ♩♪)

2. I'm goin' where the folks all know me well, my sweet baby,
   Goin' where the folks all know me well,
   When I'm gone to my long, lonesome home.

3. So, who will be your honey when I'm gone, my sweet baby,
   Who will be your honey when I'm gone,
   When I'm gone to my long, lonesome home?

© 1993 Music Sales Corporation (ASCAP)
International Copyright Secured. All Rights Reserved.

Solo Technique

Blues guitarists usually include a full-verse solo in an arrangement of a song. The harmonic pattern of the solo follows that of the song itself. Some solos even last for several verses. A blues guitar solo is made up of different riffs that work well together as a whole. Most blues solos are based on the pentatonic blues scale. Here is a pattern for a scale in A that moves up the neck a bit.

Try playing each of these A pentatonic blues riffs now.

Riff 1

Riff 2

Riff 3

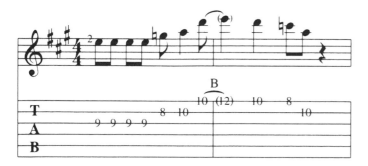

Once you can play these riffs, string them together into one twelve-bar section. Increase and decrease your level of volume and expression according to the rise and fall of the three *phrase marks*.

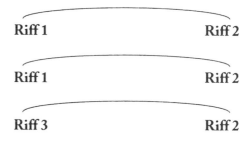

Here's how the twelve-bar blues progression corresponds with this riff pattern.

I	-	I
IV	-	I
V - IV	-	I

As you can see, Riffs 1 and 2 are played over a I chord, Riff 1 also works well with the IV chord, and Riff 3 moves nicely from the V to the IV chord. Because of the all-purpose quality of the blues scale, many riffs are actually interchangeable. Here are two riffs that work equally well with both I and IV chords. The short slides at the beginning of the first riff should start from one or two frets below the written note.

Now play "Stagolee" in the key of A. Use the indicated strum, or your own variations, during the verse sections. Play the one-verse solo as written after Verse 2 of the song. Focus on increasing and decreasing your volume and expression to bring out each four-bar phrase—and to give the solo a definite beginning and ending. You can play the solo again after Verse 4, or create one of your own using a different combination of these riffs.

Stagolee

Medium shuffle (♩♩ = ♩ ♪)

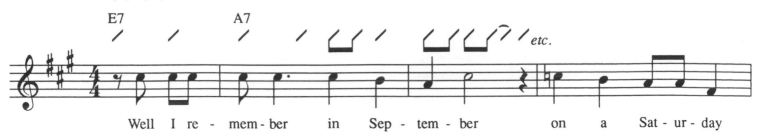

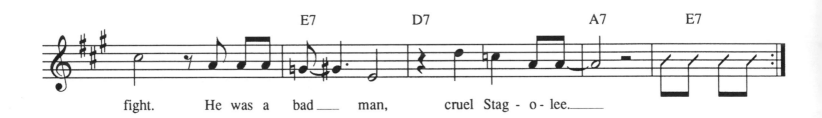

Well I re - mem - ber in Sep - tem - ber on a Sat - ur - day night, Stag - o - lee ___ and Bil - ly Lyons ___ had a great fight. He was a bad ___ man, cruel Stag - o - lee. ___

2. Stagolee shot Billy Lyons—what do you think of that?
   Shot him down in cold blood 'cause he stole his Stetson hat.
   He was a bad man, cruel Stagolee.
   Solo

3. Billy Lyons said, "Stagolee, please don't take my life,
   I've got two little babies and a darling, loving wife.
   You are a bad man, cruel Stagolee."

4. "What do I care for your babies or your darling, loving wife?
   You done stole my Stetson—I'm bound to take your life."
   He was a bad man, cruel Stagolee.
   Solo

5. Two o'clock next Tuesday, upon a scaffold high,
   People came from miles around to watch old Stagolee die.
   He was a bad man, cruel Stagolee.

© 1993 Music Sales Corporation (ASCAP)
International Copyright Secured. All Rights Reserved.

Solo

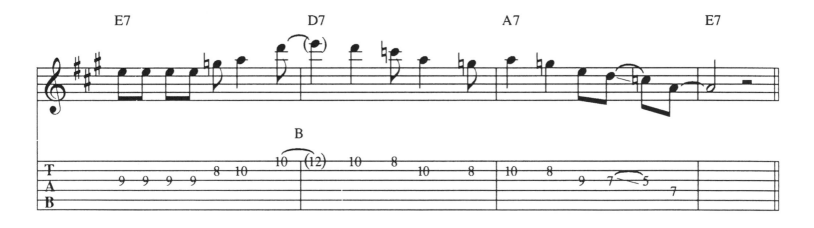

Improvising Riffs

You can improvise your own fills, turnarounds, and solos by shaping blues riffs into phrases. Once you learn a specific lick, try inventing a variation by changing the rhythm or pitch of the notes. Or, lengthen a given riff to create an extended variation. You have seen how blues lines are based on the pentatonic blues scale. Now play an extended version—the seven-note *E blues scale*.

You can improvise many different kinds of riffs to complement the melody line of a given blues song. In fact, many blues artists are known for their ability to weave the vocal and guitar lines together in this way. Compare the first line of "Midnight Special" with two riffs which are based on this melody. Note that the first riff imitates (or echoes) the vocal line. The second riff reverses (or mirrors) the vocal line. Both riffs make great fills that "answer" the "question" posed by the melody.

Well, you get up in the morn-ing,

Some improvised riffs simply center around a special effect. This one uses slides and repeated notes.

Now play "Midnight Special" using the indicated riffs. This old-time blues memorializes the midnight run of the *Golden Gate Limited*, whose engine headlight could be seen by inmates of the Texas State Prison. This song uses an eight-bar blues form in a verse-verse-chorus pattern. Once you can play this arrangement smoothly, try improvising your own fills.

Midnight Special

© 1993 Music Sales Corporation (ASCAP)
International Copyright Secured. All Rights Reserved.

2. Well, if you're ever down in Houston,
   You'd better walk on by,
   Oh, you'd better not gamble,
   And, you'd better not fight.
   Because the sheriff will arrest you,
   His boys will pull you down,
   And then, before you know it,
   You're penitentiary bound.
   Chorus

3. Yonder comes Miss Lucy.
   How in the world do you know?
   I can tell her by her apron,
   And the dress she wore.
   Umbrella on her shoulder,
   Piece of paper in her hand,
   She's gonna see the sheriff,
   To try and free her man.
   Chorus

Minor Blues

So far you have played blues songs in major keys which contain a few minor chords. Blues songs written in a *minor key* feature minor chords primarily—and have a dark and mournful sound. You are already familiar with the three basic chords in the key of A minor—Am, Dm, and E7. The F7 and C chords are also frequently used in the key of A minor.

F

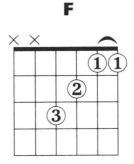

F7   **C**

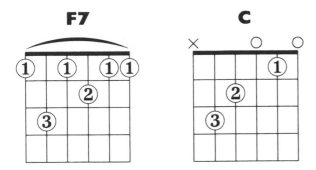

Once you are familiar with these chords, play "St. James Infirmary," a traditional eight-bar minor blues. This grim tale of personal loss is a standard in the repertoire of blues and jazz musicians alike. Explore the suggested intro, turnarounds, solo section, and ending as you develop your personal arrangement of this song. Bends, slides, hammerons, and pulloffs add expression to this bluesy guitar solo, which works very nicely after Verse 2 and/or Verse 5.

You can improvise your own turnarounds and solos based on the A pentatonic blues scale (which works in both major and minor keys). You can find the basic chords for other minor keys in the "Table of Blues Chords" at the end of this book.

The F7 chord shown above is called a *bar chord*, because you must use your index finger as a "bar" to fret all six strings at the first fret. The F chord shown below is easier to play and may be used in place of the F7 chord. However, it really pays to know both versions.

St. James Infirmary

© 1993 Music Sales Corporation (ASCAP)
International Copyright Secured. All Rights Reserved.

Solo

* An R *means to release the bend you are holding.*

Turnarounds

Ending

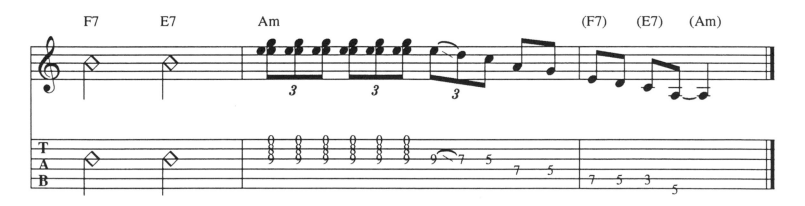

2. I went up to see the doctor,
   "She's very low," he said.
   I went back to see my baby,
   And, good God, she was lying there dead.

3. I went down to old Joe's barroom
   On the corner by the square,
   The drinks were served as usual,
   And the usual crowd was there.

4. On my left stood Joe MacKennedy,
   His eyes were bloodshot red,
   He turned to the crowd around him,
   And these are the words he said:

5. Let her go, let her go, God bless her,
   Wherever she may be.
   She may search this wide world over,
   But never find another man like me.

6. Now when I die, please bury me
   In a high-top Stetson hat,
   Put a gold piece on my watch chain,
   So the gang will know I'm standing pat.

7. And now that you've heard my story,
   I'll take another shot of booze,
   If anyone should happen to ask you,
   I've got the St. James Infirmary blues.

24

Country Blues

The Mississippi Delta region was home to many early blues writers and musicians. As the blues spread throughout Texas and the South, it took on many characteristics of other existing Southern folk music. This produced a wide range of regional styles, collectively known as *country blues*. Fingerpicking is an important playing technique for many country blues guitarists. To play this style, you must keep a steady bassline going with your thumb and then add some treble notes with your index and middle fingers (*p*=thumb, *i*=index, and *m*=middle). Try playing this traditional alternating bass pattern, which moves from an E chord to an A7 chord.

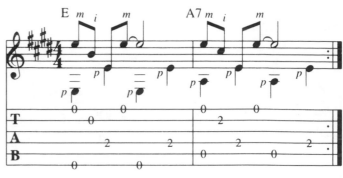

You can get a different country feel by adding *thumb brushes* to the alternating bass pattern. To get this effect, just brush down across two or three strings instead of playing a single bass note on beats 2 and 4 of the bassline. (A thumb brush is indicated by an arrow next to the brushed notes.) Use thumb brushes as you play this pattern, moving from an A7 chord to a B7 chord.

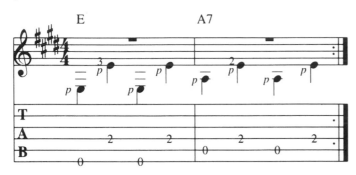

Now try adding some treble notes. The first note in each measure falls on the beat and, along with the first bass note, is called a *pinch*. The other two notes fall in between beats.

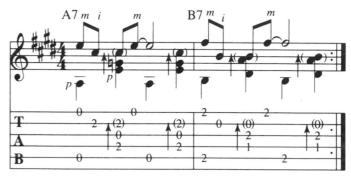

Now play "Risin' River Blues" using this pattern. Notice that variations on this picking pattern are used in the introduction and ending of this traditional country blues to add movement and interest to the arrangement.

Risin' River Blues

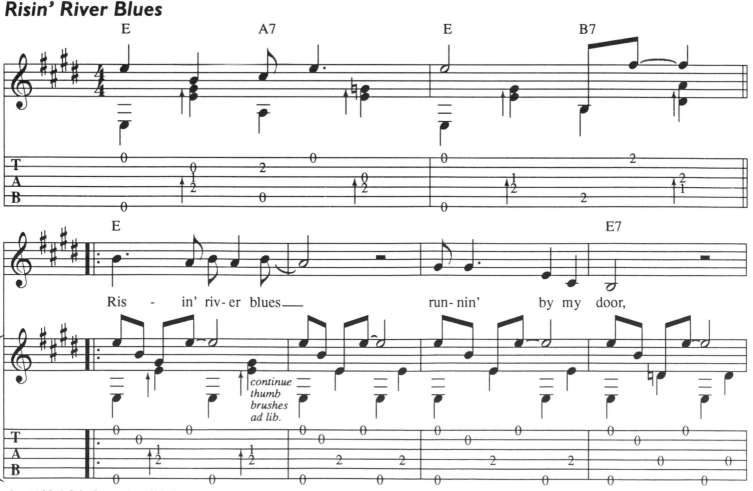

Ris - in' riv-er blues___ run-nin' by my door,

continue
thumb
brushes
ad lib.

© 1993 Music Sales Corporation (ASCAP)
International Copyright Secured. All Rights Reserved.

Come here, sweet mama, let me speak my mind,
Come here, sweet mama, let me speak my mind,
To cure these blues, gonna take a long, long time.

Jazz Blues

Jazz developed in the early part of this century as a natural outgrowth of the blues. In fact, many an early jazz tune was nothing more than a blues song with an expanded structure and harmony. The typical *jazz blues* song required a more sophisticated chord progression than the traditional blues form. These additional chords gave the jazz blues song that characteristic "ragtime" sound and helped the song to sustain a larger overall structure. For example, the "St. Louis Blues" is written in three sections—and requires several new chords in the key of G, as shown below. Practice each of these chords until you can change smoothly from one to another.

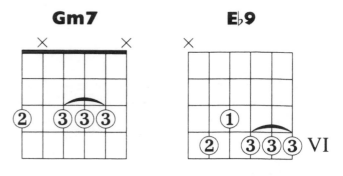

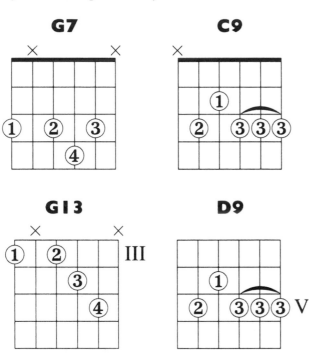

W.C. Handy (sometimes called "the father of the blues") wrote the music and lyrics to "St. Louis Blues" in 1914. Since then, this song has enjoyed worldwide popularity—and even inspired a musical film of the same name in 1928 featuring Bessie Smith. A favorite number of Louis Armstrong and other jazz performers, this sophisticated jazz blues features a powerful chromatic melody line and some interesting syncopated rhythms. Use relatively short, crisp strokes as you strum the chords to this one in a steady rhythm.

St. Louis Blues

© 1993 Music Sales Corporation (ASCAP)
International Copyright Secured. All Rights Reserved.

Rock Blues

Rock and roll owes its heritage to the blues. In fact, many rock artists have created popular hits using traditional blues songs. "Crossroad Blues" was a favorite of blues master Robert Johnson. In 1969, Cream did a classic blues-rock version of this great twelve-bar blues. For the intro and fill sections of "Crossroads," Eric Clapton plays a driving riff made up of notes taken from a first-position A blues scale. Practice this scale now.

Now play this riff, which features a pulloff followed by a hammeron. Fret the A note on the third string, second fret using your second finger. Play the note, then pluck the string with your left-hand second finger to sound the open third string. Then replace your second finger on the third string, second fret to play the third note.

Now try the whole riff. If you are playing with a pick, use downstrokes (⊓) and upstrokes (V) as indicated. If you are playing with your fingers, use your thumb to play the low A notes on the open fifth string and pick the treble notes with alternating index and middle fingers.

The solo makes use of the "sliding-scale" version of the A pentatonic scale that you used in "Stagolee" and "St. James Infirmary," with the addition of one note. This six-note scale is an extremely common and useful variation of the blues scale, which you can use as a basis for riffs and solos. Practice this six-note scale form now.

At the beginning of the solo, you'll see a wavy line above the whole-note A (tenth fret, second string). This symbol indicates *vibrato*.

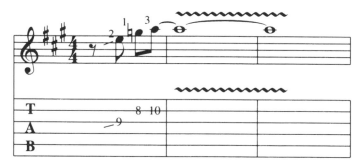

As you hold the note, shake your hand back and forth in line with the guitar neck. This produces a slight variation in pitch and intensity of the held note. For a more pronounced type of vibrato, you can shake your finger up and down (perpendicular to the neck). Experiment with these two types of vibrato at different speeds and levels of intensity as you are learning this blues-rock solo.

Try coming up with your own intro, fills, and solo for "Crossroads." Experiment with mixing the two scale forms and finding the right places for hammerons, pulloffs, slides, bends, and vibrato. Feel free to make a note of the riffs that work best as you put together your own blues-rock arrangement of this classic song.

Crossroad Blues

© 1993 Music Sales Corporation (ASCAP)
International Copyright Secured. All Rights Reserved.

Standing there at the crossroads, tried to flag a ride,
Standing there at the crossroads, tried to flag a ride,
Nobody there seemed to know me, they just passed me by.

Table of Blues Scales

This section includes the popular six-note blues scale in every key. As a general rule, blues guitarists favor the keys of A, E, D, and G. However, you may need to transpose a given song on the spot when you are working with other musicians. For instance, many clarinet, sax, and trumpet players favor flat keys because of the tuning of their instruments. Similarly, a singer may need a piece to be transposed to suit his or her particular vocal range. To avoid repetition in this table, scales which sound exactly alike (called *enharmonic equivalents*) are shown in the more common key. (For example, to play a C♭ blues scale, use the fingering shown for the key of B.)

A Blues Scale

You are already familiar with this scale, which is shown on page 45.

B♭ Blues Scale

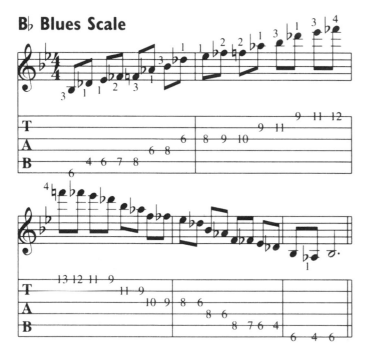

B (or C♭) Blues Scale

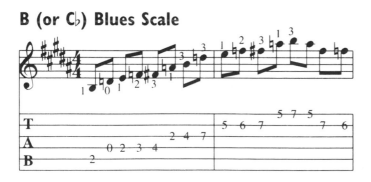

C Blues Scale

D♭ (or C♯) Blues Scale

D Blues Scale

Eb Blues Scale

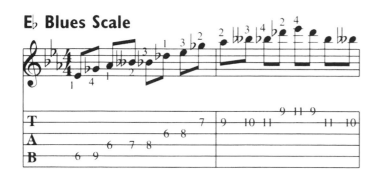

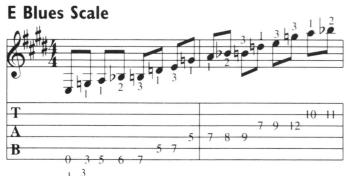

E Blues Scale

F Blues Scale

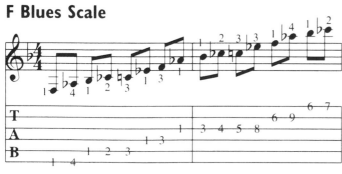

F# (or Gb) Blues Scale

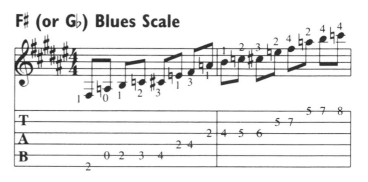

G Blues Scale

Ab Blues Scale

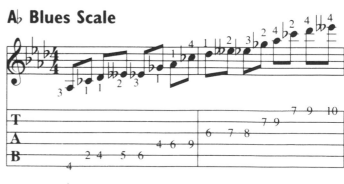

Table of Blues Chords

In the following pages, you will find the most commonly used blues chords in all major and minor keys. Here are some basic progressions you can use to play different versions of the blues in the key of your choice.

Standard 8-Bar Blues

I	I7	IV	I
V7	V7	I - IV7	I

Standard 12-Bar Blues

I	I	I	I7
IV7	IV7	I	I
V7	V7	I	I

12-Bar Blues Variation

I	IV7	I	I7
IV7	IVm	I	I7
V7	IV7	I	I

Minor 12-Bar Blues

Im7	Im7	Im7	Im7
IVm	IVm	Im	Im7
V7	IVm	Im7	Im7

Minor 12-Bar Blues Variation

Im7	IVm - V7	Im7	I7
IVm	IVm - V9	Im7	I7
IVm	♭VI7 - V9	Im7	Im7

Use these two-measure progressions to play a basic blues intro, turnaround, or ending in any major key.

Intro

| I | ♭VI7 | V7 | |

Turnaround

| I I7 IV IVm | I ♭VI7 V7 | |

Ending

| I | IV7 ♭VI7 | I | I7 |

Use these two-measure progressions to play a basic blues intro, turnaround, or ending in any minor key.

Intro

| Im7 | IVm | V7 ♭VI7 V7 | |

Turnaround

| Im Im7 IVm ♭VI7 | V7 ♭VI7 V7 | |

Ending

| Im7 | IVm V9 | Im7 | |

Key of A

I	I7	IV7	V7
A	**A7**	**D7**	**E7**

Im7	IVm	V9	♭VI7
Am7	**Dm**	**E9**	**F7**

Key of B♭

I	I7	IV7	V7
B♭	**B♭7**	**E♭7**	**F7**

Im7	IVm	V9	♭VI7
B♭m7	**E♭m**	**F9**	**G♭7**

Key of B (or C♭)

I	I7	IV7	V7
B	**B7**	**E7**	**F♯7**

Im7	IVm	V9	♭VI7
Bm7	**Em**	**F♯9**	**G7**

Key of C

I	I7	IV7	V7
C	**C7**	**F7**	**G7**

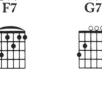

Im7	IVm	V9	♭VI7
Cm7	**Fm**	**G9**	**A♭7**

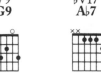

Key of D♭ (or C♯)

Key of D

Key of E♭

Key of E

Key of F

Key of F♯ (or G♭)

Key of G

Key of A♭